Inspiring Thoughts for Your Marriage

This is a complete list of books by Charles L. Allen since he became a Revell author in 1951.

God's Psychiatry
The Touch of the Master's Hand
All Things Are Possible Through Prayer
When You Lose a Loved One
When the Heart Is Hungry
The Twenty-third Psalm
The Ten Commandments
The Lord's Prayer
The Beatitudes
Twelve Ways to Solve Your Problems
Healing Words
The Life of Christ
Prayer Changes Things
The Sermon on the Mount
Life More Abundant
The Charles L. Allen Treasury (with Charles L. Wallis)
Roads to Radiant Living
Riches of Prayer
In Quest of God's Power
When You Graduate (with Mouzon Biggs)
The Miracle of Love
The Miracle of Hope
The Miracle of the Holy Spirit
Christmas in Our Hearts (with Charles L. Wallis)
Candle, Star and Christmas Tree (with Charles L. Wallis)
When Christmas Came to Bethlehem (with Charles L. Wallis)
Christmas (with Charles L. Wallis)
What I Have Lived By
You Are Never Alone
Perfect Peace
How to Increase Your Sunday-School Attendance (with Mildred Parker)
The Secret of Abundant Living
Victory in the Valleys of Life
Faith, Hope, and Love
Joyful Living
Inspiring Thoughts for Your Marriage

Charles L. Allen

Inspiring Thoughts for Your Marriage

Fleming H. Revell Company
Old Tappan, New Jersey

Unless otherwise identified, Scripture quotations are from the King James Version of the Bible.

Scripture quotations identified RSV are from the Revised Standard Version of the Bible, copyrighted 1946, 1952, © 1971 and 1973.

"Useless Words," by Carl Sandburg, from GOOD MORNING, AMERICA, copyright 1928, 1956 by Carl Sandburg. Reprinted by permission of Harcourt Brace Jovanovich, Inc.

Quotations from MAKING YOUR MARRIAGE SUCCEED, by Theodore F. Adams used by permission of John J. Adams.

Quotation from "LET THE REST OF THE WORLD GO BY"
J. Keirn Brennan and Ernest R. Ball
© 1919 (renewed) Warner Bros. Inc.
All rights reserved.
Used by permission.

Library of Congress Cataloging in Publication Data

Allen, Charles Livingstone, 1913–
    Inspiring thoughts for your marriage.

    1. Marriage—Religious aspects—Christianity.
2. Marriage—Meditations.   I. Title.
BV835.A45   1985   248.4   84–24872
ISBN 0-8007-1401-6

TO

Alice and David C. Bintliff

Whose beautiful marriage began January 17, 1923 and whose lives inspire their wonderful children and grandchildren, me, and many, many others

Contents

Inspiring Thoughts for Your Marriage

1 The Marriage Emotion

When does the marriage emotion begin in a person? The answer is very, very, very early.

Once, while I was observing children in a church nursery, a little boy came over and began pushing a little girl. Seeing this, another little boy said, "Don't do dat." The first little boy pushed the little girl a second time, whereupon the other little boy began hitting him as hard as he could with his fists, saying, "I told you, 'Don't do dat.' "

In those two-year-old children I saw that the marriage emotion had already strongly implanted itself in them. Watch little children play together, and very soon we see the boy become the defender, the soldier, the policeman, the one who protects. The little girl takes care of her doll as though it were her own child. She plays the part of the mother and the homemaker. She will set the table and act as if she were fixing dinner.

As children grow older, there comes a period in their lives when they seem not to like the opposite sex; boys like to be with boys, and girls like to be with girls. However, that period does not last very long, and life takes on new glamour and enthusiasm as young boys and young girls begin to notice each other.

Teenage boys and girls almost instinctively pair off with each other. The boy-girl relationship is very different from the boy-boy or the girl-girl relationship. Sometimes children and teenagers hear, "You are too young." But almost no child is too young to want friendship and popularity. Few children are too young to "play house," to dream of being papa and mama, to feel love for some person of the opposite sex. Very early in life, do the deep and surging sex instincts and emotions make themselves felt. Deep inside something in every person makes one want comradeship with another. These instincts and urges are God given, and long before they ever read the words in the Bible, young people experience the feelings of which Jesus spoke:

> *For this cause shall a man leave father and mother, and shall cleave to his wife: and they twain shall be one flesh? Wherefore they are no more twain, but one flesh. What therefore God hath joined together, let not man put asunder.*

> *Matthew 19:5, 6*

Benjamin Franklin said well:

> *It is a man and a woman united that makes the complete human being. Separate, she wants his force of body and strength of reason. He wants her softness, her sensitiveness, her acute discerning. Together they are more likely to succeed than apart.*

When we are very young we want to love and be loved. We love our parents, our brothers and sisters, but something about loving one of the opposite sex brings a very special joy and a satisfaction. Sometimes we call it "puppy love." As young people we experience exciting days when we love someone, even if it is only for a week or a month, then somebody else the next week, the next month. That is part of the emotional development that goes into the life of a growing person. Through those days we learn that there are different kinds of love. There is the impersonal love, such as the love of your country, your school. Then there is the love between parent and child and between brother and sister. There is fraternal love that one feels for other members of the class or for friends in the Boy Scout or Girl Scout troop or other group relationships. Finally there is that deep mating love in every normal human being, which is so essential to marriage. Mating love begins early in life and it continues to grow throughout the balance of one's life. Mating love is one of the greatest of all of life's inspirations. Many years ago an unknown author said it this way:

> *I love you,*
> *Not only for what you are,*
> *But for what I am*
> *When I am with you.*
>
> *I love you,*
> *Not only for what*
> *You have made of yourself,*
> *But for what you are making of me.*
>
> *I love you*
> *For the part of me*
> *That you bring out;*
> *I love you*
> *For putting your hand*
> *Into my heaped up heart*
> *And passing over*
> *All the foolish, weak things*
> *That you cannot help*
> *Dimly seeing there,*
> *And drawing out*
> *Into the light*
> *All the beautiful belongings*
> *That no one else has looked*
> *Quite far enough to find.*
>
> *I love you because you*
> *Are helping me to make*
> *Of the lumber of my life*
> *Not a tavern*
> *But a temple;*
> *Out of the works*
> *Of my every day*
> *Not a reproach*
> *But a song.*

As we look back in life to our earliest beginnings we can think of many people with whom we felt we fell in love. Sometimes it was love for just a day or week or maybe a month. Those sudden infatuations came and went, but they were very moving experiences. Popularity, good looks, physical prowess, hero worship, and many other causes enhanced them. During them, one could feel such emotions as insecurity, wishful thinking, loss of appetite, and general security. All these emotions are part of the growing process of romantic love. And as that love grows, eventually we come to realize that true love brings a growing sense of security and well-being. Gradually our infatuations grow into true love, which can endure the trials, difficulties, and disappointments of life. "Now abideth faith, hope, and love, these three; and the greatest of these is love" (*see* 1 Corinthians 13:13).

Love is so rich and so deep that when it really comes, it takes all that you are and all of your life to express its full meaning.

> *... Love is strong as death. ... Many waters cannot quench love, neither can the floods drown it. ...*
>
> Song of Solomon 8:6, 7

> *The most wonderful of all things in life, I believe, is the discovery of another human being with whom one's relationship has a glowing depth, beauty, and joy as the years increase. This inner progressiveness of love between human beings is a most marvelous thing, it cannot be found by looking for it or by passionately wishing for it. It is a sort of divine accident.*
>
> HUGH WALPOLE

> *Since "I love you" may simply mean, in all sorts of subtle ways, "I love me and want you," since such love need not at all change its ulterior purpose in loving in order to want another in the same supposed interest of self-fulfillment, a person had better subject his love to this severe testing; see if he can promise permanence in love for another person precisely under*

those conditions referred to in the expressions, "for worse," "for poorer," and "in sickness," under which he will have to give rather than to derive benefit from the marriage relationship.

> *PAUL RAMSEY*
> Basic Christian Ethics

When Jane Burdon first sat for William Morris, the artist spent some time before his canvas and at last showed it to the model. Instead of a picture the canvas bore the words; "I cannot paint you but I love you."

> *NORMAN GOODALL*
> One Man's Testimony

2 How to Know You Are Really in Love

Here are some questions to begin with:

Is he or she physically attractive to you?

Do you share some undisputed common tastes, ideals, and standards?

Do you have a feeling of unrest and even of unhappiness when you are separated or not in contact with each other?

Do you really want to consider the other one's opinions or desires as well as your own?

Are you happier when you are with him or her than when you are with anyone else?

When you are together, do you always insist on having your way, or is there a willingness to give and take between you? Does he or she bring out the best that is within you and make you want to be a better person?

Do you have common interests, and do you like to do things together?

Do you trust each other and have faith in each other's character?

Would you like your child to be like him or her?

Are you willing to give up your own preferences in order to please him or her?

Is there anything in him or her of which you are ashamed or feel the need to apologize for?

Even when you disagree, can you still be agreeable?

As you look at life do you think in terms of both of you, rather than of just yourself, alone?

Are there some people whom you both consider as friends?

When there is a pain or a difficulty, can you feel pulled together or pushed apart?

In the play *The Hasty Heart,* a soldier has been a hospital patient for a long time. He asks his nurse to marry him. She has done a lot for him, and he really feels not only gratitude, but a sense of obligation. He tells her how much he is indebted to her. She wonders whether he really loves her or simply feels obligated to her. She asks him the question, and he answers very clearly, "I give you my heart because it is no good to me without you." Only that type of love and devotion can really be a foundation for marriage.

How do you know you are in love? Courtship is one step on the road to happiness and marriage. This wonderful experience not only leads to marriage, courtship should continue to the very end of marriage, never ceasing.

There is a wonderful story of a couple who were on their honeymoon. One day she exclaimed to him, "Darling, isn't this heaven?"

He replied, "Do you know, life does not seem long enough for our happiness. Just think, even if we are very fortunate, our married life can hardly last much longer than fifty years!"

"Is that all?" she questioned, edging a little closer to him.

"Yes," he replied, "only a little more than fifty years in which to love each other."

"Then kiss me quickly, dear," she said. "We are wasting time!"

Courtship gives us time to grow and to realize the kind of person we really want to marry. It gives us time to know the other and to make a reasonable judgment if this is the person with whom we want to live the rest of our lives. There is a poem that expressed the feelings of many people:

> There was a lad when I was young
> I worshipped in such wise
> Name was honey on my tongue;
> Smile, my paradise.
>
> He was nimble-footed, bold,
> And beautiful to see.
> But, oh, his prideful heart was cold
> Concerning love and me.
>
> So night on night I prayed and cried
> To win for my dear

Thank heaven, God was occupied
With someone else that year.

THEODORE F. ADAMS
Making Your Marriage Succeed

Courtship gives us a chance to be certain we have made the right decision. Through the time we spend with a special person, we grow. We better understand our goals, purposes, and ideals in life. We seek God's guidance to arrive at the right choice.

Love has many sides that all work together to help us choose the right mate. Perhaps the most talked about one is the physical aspect of love. Naturally lovers feel attracted to each other, but this alone is not enough to make a happy marriage.

Lovers also need to have some matching experiences—we might call this the mental side of love. We need to share common interests and a growing understanding. Learning to plan and think together forms an important part of the courtship period.

Another obvious facet of love is the feeling side of it. Through contact before marriage, we find out if we are happy in each other's presence and miserable during separations. Courtship should be a time of acceptance and well-being and we should feel uplifted, not put down.

Are you really in love? As you consider that question, if you can seriously ask "Is it possible to love two people at the same time?" stop right there. Courtship means loving *one* person all the time. We commit ourselves to love that other person, and we say it. We begin to understand whether that person is more interested in what he or she can do for us or in what he or she can get out of us. And we communicate our attitude toward our beloved, too.

We prove our love in many ways: We love each other even though we may be separated for periods of time; we generously consider each other's feelings, wishes, and desires; we meet and get to know each other's families. And during courtship others will see our love for each other. Love cannot be hidden. As we express our feelings our friends see and know it.

Together we begin to dream together, and we see goals to strive for. There is a story about Matthew Henry, the great Bible scholar. As a young ministerial student, he fell in love with a girl who was very wealthy and cultured. Her father said to her, "I do not think you ought to have anything more to do with that young man. We do not know anything about his family or his background or where he came from." The girl replied firmly, "Yes, but father, I know where he is going, and I am going to go with him."

In these days before marriage we decide where we are going and if we want to go there together. We measure how much emotional tension each one can carry without spilling over. We learn if we can face the tensions of life as mature people.

Have we outgrown childish and foolish anxieties? Little children might be afraid of the dark or of loud noises or of being different from other people, but as we become emotionally mature, we can expect to treat and be treated as responsible partners in marriage. A man or woman might expect a spouse to "mother" or "father" him or her. Now we need to realize that we are not babies any longer, but are ready to settle down to the realities of life, of making a home, rearing a family, and being responsible citizens in our society.

> *THEODORE: "But if you love him, my dear, marriage brings together those who love truly."*
>
> *HELEN: "But those who love each other truly, don't need anything to bring them together. The difficulty is to keep them apart."*

JESSIE LYNCH WILLIAM
Why Marry?

> *"The point is we are married—married. Doesn't that mean something to you, something—inexorable? It does to me. I didn't dream it would—in just that way. But all I can say is that I suppose the people who don't feel it aren't really married."*

EDITH WHARTON
The Glimpses of the Moon

> *It's man that marries for a home—a home that, having got it, superficially he cares little enough about, and superficially uses it as a good place to get away from—that's what he marries for—a home; a place to bring his things to and wherein to keep his things; an establishment; a solid anchored*

base; a place where he can have his wife and his children and his dog and his book—and his treasures and his slippers and his ease, and can feel, comfortably, she and they and yet are here.

A. S. M. HUTCHISON
This Freedom

Intense love of a man and his wife means that the soul is attuned to all that is beautiful in love. Herein is the secret of God's great love. We sometimes think the universe itself is so immense that God cannot give peculiar care to the individual. But Jesus says that God did not build man for the universe but the universe for man. God could not love the world without loving the individual. It is idle to speak of loving humanity but refusing to love each other as persons. We must first choose the narrow way, and as we come to that place that we love one person more than we love any other person, then it is our love begins to reach out in love for all persons.

FRED R. CHENAULT
Christian Herald

Love does not die easily. It is a living thing. It thrives in the face of all life's hazards, save one—neglect.

JAMES D. BRYDEN
Presbyterian Life

Infantile love follows the principle; "I love because I am loved." Mature love follows the principle; "I am loved because I love." Immature love says; "I love you because I need you." Mature love says; "I need you because I love you."

ERICH FROMM
The Art of Loving

Persons ought to be loved; things ought to be used.

REUEL POWELL

3 Romance and Marriage

In the first book of the Bible, we read these words, "Then Isaac brought her into the tent, and took Rebecca, and she became his wife; and he loved her . . ." (*see* Genesis 24:67). The story of Isaac and Rebecca is one of the earliest romances on record. In our society today couples "fall in love" and then marry, but in earlier times couples married and then fell in love. Marriages were arranged by the parents. Today young people freely choose their own mates. However it is still true that growth in mutual love is much greater after marriage than before marriage.

Our modern novels and motion-picture houses and television sets only play the story of courtship and the excitement of conquest. When the romantic game is over, marriage may happen, but then it may not. Some people feel that, after the game, everybody loses interest. We have a tendency to think in terms of "marriage" on the one hand—on the other hand of "love." Love, romance, and marriage must never be separated. We need to keep them together.

Marriage means two people are committed to a permanent sharing of life at all levels. In no other human relationship do people share both their bodies and their hearts with each other. To enter into this experience requires both courage and faith in each other. Tragically many people share the same house, but really live apart. Many couples find themselves unable to face the intimacies of marriage. In true marriage couples put away shame and false modesty and accept each other as they accept themselves—as they are. The sense of belonging to each other brings rich and satisfying rewards.

A couple talked together, and one asked the other, "What kind of person are you expecting to marry?" The other person waxed eloquently about a person who would be a combination of a movie star, a literary genius, a perfect physical body, deep and understanding love, and all the other qualities one could dream of. Then quietly the other one asked, "And just what do you have to offer in return?" Happily, for a couple to be successfully and lovingly married, neither need be great or perfect. The extremely essential element is that couples accept each other. Many people feel that acceptance is more important than even love. We do not marry each other to reform each other but we must accept each other.

Many years ago Dr. Roy Burkhart wrote a book entitled *From Friendship to Marriage.* He told about asking 500 happy and 500 unhappy married couples what they thought were the most important qualities if the home is to succeed. These couples listed twelve important qualities:

> A congenial spirit
> A noncritical attitude
> Supreme satisfaction in making the other happy
> Good health
> Physical and emotional maturity
> Love of children
> The same religion
> Similar economic backgrounds
> Similar social backgrounds
> The ability to combat one's own moods and overlook the other's mistakes
> Cleanliness
> Neatness

We all know happily married couples who have not had all twelve qualities. Couples with different backgrounds have become very happy together. However, in courtship and as we accept each other, we develop a sense of security, and upon that secure feeling we build our marriage and our home. Thank goodness we do not have to find the "perfect" partner. If we did, there would be very few marriages. Many people can identify the feelings of the girl described in the following verses:

> *At sweet sixteen, I first began*
> *To ask the Good Lord for a man;*
> *At seventeen, I recall,*
> *I wanted someone strong and tall.*
> *At Christmas I reached eighteen*
> *Fancied someone blonde and lean.*
> *Then at nineteen, I was sure*
> *I'd fall for someone more mature.*
> *At twenty I thought I'd find*
> *Romance with someone with a mind.*
> *I retrogressed at twenty-one*
> *And found college boys most fun.*
> *My viewpoint changed at twenty-two,*
> *When "one man only" was my cue.*
> *Broke my heart at twenty-three*
> *And asked for someone kind to me.*
> *And then at blasé twenty-four*
> *For anyone who wouldn't bore;*
> *Now, Lord, I am twenty-five*
> *Just send me someone who's alive.*

THEODORE F. ADAMS
Making Your Marriage Succeed

Someone has well said, "Husbands fall into three classes: prizes, surprises, and consolation prizes." The same might be said of wives. Each husband and wife is likely to get someone about on his or her level. Neither of them is perfect, but both of them can be truly wonderful for each other.

We frequently read and hear of qualities "essential" to success and marriage. Many are important, but in almost no marriage do all the ideal qualities exist. And almost none of them are absolutely essential. Love and romance in marriage can overcome the lack of "necessary" qualities such as knowing each other for two or more years, having a long engagement, attending the same church, similar family background, adequate marriage counseling, a good relationship with the in-laws, physical health, and so on.

It is said that an optimist is one who makes the best of it when he gets the worst of it.

> SHE: *"You remind me of the ocean."*
> HE: *"Loud, restless, and romantic?"*
> SHE: *"No. You just make me sick."*

Then shall the minister say unto the man, Wilt thou have this woman to be thy wedded wife . . . and forsaking all others, keep thee only unto her, so long as ye both shall live? . . . and unto the woman, Wilt thou have this man to thy wedded husband. . . . and forsaking all others, keep thee only unto him so long as ye both shall live? It is a formidable decision to make when one says, "I bind myself for life! I have chosen: From now on my aim will be, not to search for someone who may please me, but to please the one I have chosen." Yet this decision can alone produce a successful marriage, and if the vow is not sincere the couple's chances for happiness are very slim, for it will run the risk of disruption when the first obstacles and the inevitable difficulties of life in common are encountered.

ANDRE MAUROIS
The Art of Living

The grave of Charles Kingsley in Eversley Churchyard is marked by a white marble cross on which are the chosen words: Amavimus, amamus, amabimus (*We have loved. We love. We shall love.*)

"Love," said Francis of Assisi, "sets my heart ablaze."

All the world loves a lover, God loves us all and we love Him! Love is a word—a shameless raged ghost of a word—begging at all doors for life at any price!

EUGENE O'NEILL
The God Brown

*Love is the passionate and abiding desire on the part of two
people . . . to produce the conditions under which each can be
and spontaneously express his real self; to produce together an
intellectual soil and an emotional climate in which can flourish,
far superior to what each could achieve alone.*

ALEXANDER MAGOUN
Love and Marriage

*In his autobiography, Calvin Coolidge, the former presi-
dent, wrote in these words concerning the girl he married,
Grace Goodhue: "From our being together we seemed naturally to come to care for each other. We became engaged in the
early summer of 1905 and were married. . . . on October 4th
of that year. I have seen so much fiction written on this subject
that I may be pardoned for relating the plain facts. We
thought we were made for each other. For almost a quarter of
a century she has borne with my infirmities, and I have re-
joiced in her graces."*

*On the occasion of his retirement from Riverside Church,
Harry Emerson Fosdick said he had been puzzled all his life by
the fact that on the whole, women have not accomplished as
much in a public way as has been accomplished by men. Why
is this true? Obviously the brains of women are as good and
perhaps better than the brains of men. Yet the sober truth
is that there have been relatively few women in the lists of
composers, artists, scientists, and statesmen. "At last,"
said Dr. Fosdick, "I know the answer. No woman ever
had a wife."*

To be happy at home is the ultimate result of all ambition.

SAMUEL JOHNSON

When the one man loves the one woman and the one woman loves the one man, the very angels leave heaven and come sit in that house and sing for you.

BRAHMA

The highest happiness on earth is in marriage. Every man who is happily married is a successful man even if he has failed in everything else.

WILLIAM LYON PHELPS

4 Sex, Love, and Marriage

In the very first chapter of the Bible we read, "Male and female created he them. And God blessed them . . ." (Genesis 1:27, 28). One of the truly powerful forces that draws men and women together in marriage is the physical attraction. This is normal, healthy, God inspired. If God had not put into people this strong urge for each other, the function of reproduction might be so neglected that the purpose of creation would be defeated. He endowed us with an intense sexual desire. Sex is a part of our nature that can be a source of deep fulfillment and rich fruitfulness. This necessary aspect is the most tender expression of spiritual love between husband and wife. It refreshes and renews and enriches the marriage relationship. As couples begin their married lives, they learn with each other how to express their love for each other in the marvelous and wonderful union of their bodies. Such physical expression can be a deeply spiritual experience.

Our society today expresses the deep conviction that monogamy and fidelity are both fundamental and essential. We believe that marriage at its very best means one man and one woman joined together. As we see Adam and Eve it seems that is what God had in mind. Later certain societies did not believe that monogamy was the only or best way. But the experience of the centuries supports monogamy. Polygamy is really a perversion of marriage.

27

Monogamy means that husband and wife love each other and only each other. It further means that husband and wife accept each other as equals. In certain marriage ceremonies in past generations, the wife was asked to promise to "obey" her husband, while it made no corresponding demand on him. That is truly an unchristian concept and in most ceremonies today, that word is not included. God equally loves and honors all human beings. There is a place for the man and a place for the woman, but happily today, we have arrived at the place where both men and women stand equally together.

Marriage demands a commitment to fidelity. How important it is to share the experience of sexual union only with one's marriage partner! The thought of infidelity—by either the man or woman—should fill both husband and wife with horror. Having a sexual relationship outside the marriage is a concept that remains remote from the minds of true lovers. They expect faithfulness equally from both partners.

An old rabbi beautifully explained the significance of Eve's creation when he said that God made her out of Adam's rib so that she would be beneath his arm for him to protect her, close to his heart for him to love her, and at his side to walk in full equality with him. God wisely did not take a bone from Adam's hand, lest Adam use her as a tool. He did not take a bone from Adam's foot, lest he tread upon her. He did not take a bone from Adam's head, lest she try to dominate him. Out of his side a rib was taken that together they might be partners side by side for life.

Within marriage sex does not need to be, and should not be, regarded with feelings of fear, guilt, or shame. The fellowship of marriage includes sexual intimacy as a means of expressing both human love and physical desire. In times long past men spoke of their marital rights, and wives were supposed to be prepared to submit to their husbands whenever they demanded it. Happily we have passed beyond that crude and one-sided concept of marriage. Today most couples not only think of marital rights, but also of marital duties—and those duties are not so much defined by law but rather are dictated by love. Certainly no marriage partner wishes to condemn the other partner to a state of unrelieved sexual frustration. Most unresponsive husbands or wives are not that way intentionally. Oftentimes one or the other is unaware of the expression of our God-given mutual love. We need to understand it.

The sexual experience in marriage really has two functions: To unite and to procreate. As you read the Bible you do not find the procreative function of marriage emphasized, because it was both obvious and would follow automatically when the unitive function was fulfilled. In marriage sex unifies husband and wife and continuously renews and sustains that unity as they go through life together. The entire union of husband and wife must be approached with intelligence, understanding, love, and consideration. Certainly the physical factors are important, but a couple attains sexual harmony through kindness and consideration for each other.

Marital love must distinguish between love and lust. The physical experience of both love and lust seem exactly the same, and yet they are very, very different. What makes the difference between love and lust? To lust is animal; love is human. Love includes an inward spiritual quality; lust deals merely with the physical.

The term *making love* is used for sexual intercourse, and that may or may not be true. Two physical bodies cannot make love. Love is between the hearts and souls and the spirits of two people. Sexual relationship should and must express love.

In summary, the sexual relationship is normal and properly a part of marriage and should be eagerly but intelligently approached, without fear. The actual physical expression and the frequency varies with couples. But couples who remember that the ultimate in sex is making the other one happy will find fulfillment.

> *The highest and most intimate of spiritual friendships can never be marriage without the union of the flesh; but where the man and woman are one flesh, their indefinite yearnings are replaced by the peacefulness of a pervading possession, the inward energy corresponding to the outward union. Marriage is thus an ordinance peculiarly human. It is adapted to man's composite nature which is at once fleshly and spiritual.*

> *OSCAR D. WATKINS*
> Holy Matrimony

To those who are conscious of spiritual realities it seems more consonant with truth to think of love, not as derived from sex, but as an ultimate value revealed of the workings of sex. Sex is a human happening in time and space. Love is eternal in the heavens, but sex provides the medium through which love's earthly work can be accomplished, and such work is creative on all its planes.

E. D. HUTCHISON
Creative Sex

The phase of relations in which conflict first originates is that of sex. This is probably true because it is the earliest relationship demanding an adjustment.

HARRIET R. MOWRER
Personality Adjustment and
Domestic Discord

The direction and proper use of the erotic craving is one of the duties and dissipants of life. Sex is a potentiality that cannot be under-rated or trifled with, still less ignored.

WALTER M. GALLICHAN
The Psychology of Marriage

Normal sexuality as a common and similarly directed experience strengthens the feeling of unity and identity. This condition is described as one of complete harmony, and is extolled as a great happiness ("One Heart and One Soul") and with reason. It is indeed a true and undeniable experience of divinity, the transcending power which blocks out and consumes everything individual; it is a real communion.

S. G. JUNG
Contributions to Analytical Psychology

Intercourse between two people who love one another should produce not merely pleasure and satisfaction, but confidence, harmony, and self-respect. It should relieve anxiety, lessen guilt, and prevent the formation of hostility. All these consequences, being felt as a gift from the other partner, should fortify affection. To be indifferent to the physical expression of love, still more to dislike it, or to feel that it is in some way shameful, is neither superior nor virtuous nor refined; it is a symptom of mental illness or maladjustment.

AMBER BLANCO WHITE
Worry in Women

5 Marriage Is More Than a Private Affair

Couples thinking of marriage tend to consider only themselves and their own happiness. But marriage is more than a private affair. As couples develop real romantic love for each other they may experience the feeling expressed in the song:

> We'll build a sweet little nest,
> somewhere in the west,
> And let the rest of the world go by.

That concept of marriage is both escapist and immature. Normal people want social approval. We want other people to like the one we marry; we want to be proud of our mate; we want our spouse to help us in realizing our goals and ambitions in life. We want someone to help us succeed, one who is willing to share the sacrifice and dream the dreams of life.

We cannot separate that "little nest" from the world; it is a home, and a home is very much a social institution. The very foundation of our society lies not in the governing bodies of nations, but rather in our homes. The home determines what the person becomes and what the society becomes. As couples form their marriages and their homes it becomes not only something for them, but a social institution.

Someone has described a home as "the place where our bodies are fed three times a day and our souls are fed a thousand each

day." That may be true, but those three meals a day are very important.

> *Gentlemen, before you wed*
> *Ascertain how you'll be fed.*
> *Count each pan and pot*
> *That your bride to be has got.*
> *Though her kisses always please,*
> *What about her recipes?*
> *Though her glamour makes you sigh*
> *Can she bake an apple pie?*
> *Now, before it is too late,*
> *Learn your gastronomic fate.*
> *Do not trust your burning ardor*
> *'Till you've snooped around her larder.*
> *More than once has sex appeal*
> *Died with that initial meal.*

THEDORE F. ADAMS
Making Your Marriage Succeed

Not only does marriage mean the beginning of life together for two
people, it means a very different relationship must be developed between each of their families. The bride and the groom each grew up in
separate homes. Now they move out into their own home, but family
attachments remain important. When one marries, one does not neces-
sarily need to say good-bye to lifelong loved ones. Our mothers and fathers and brothers and sisters stay so the balance of our lives. Each
spouse must somehow realize that he or she not only marries the other,
each also marries the other's family. You "cut the apron strings" but
you still love your family. Marriage does not mean the end of family
relationship, but the enlargement of family relationship. Parents must
realize they must not intrude in the new home and in the new relationship.

The home is not the place where "the rest of the world goes by,"
because it forms the very foundation of religious faith. The church is a
very important institution in our society. It gives strength and support
to any couple who include the church in their lives. To belong to the
church fellowship and to worship in the holy place supports everything
that marriage stands for. However, let us remember, where religious

faith really begins. In his poem "My Altar" James H. Styles, Jr., tells us:

> *I have worshipped in churches and chapels;*
> *I've prayed in the busy street;*
> *I have sought my God and have found him*
> *Where the waves of the ocean beat;*
> *I have knelt in the silent forest*
> *In the shade of some ancient tree;*
> *But the dearest of all my altars*
> *Was raised at my mother's knee.*
>
> *I have listened to God in his temple;*
> *I've caught his voice in the crowd;*
> *I have heard him speak when the breakers*
> *Were booming long and loud;*
> *Where the winds play soft in the treetops*
> *My father has talked to me;*
> *But I never have heard him clearer*
> *Than I did at my mother's knee.*
>
> *The things in my life that are worthy*
> *Were born in my mother's breast,*
> *And breathed into mine by the magic*
> *Of the love her life expressed.*
> *The years that have brought me to manhood*
> *Have taken her far from me;*
> *But memory keeps me from straying*
> *Too far from my mother's knee.*
>
> *God, make me the man of her vision*
> *And purge me of selfishness!*
> *God, keep me true to her standards*
> *And help me to live to bless!*
> *God, hallow the holy impress*
> *Of the days that used to be,*
> *And keep me a pilgrim forever*
> *To the shrine at my mother's knee.*

When couples have a faith together it gives to them a sense of spiritual unity, and instead of withdrawing from the world, they have feeling of wanting to share their faith with other people. Religious faith is not a solitary experience, but a shared one, and the longing for the wider fellowship in the church is very satisfying. In fact, that is what the church is—a fellowship of Christian families. Having a faith, we believe that the world will be better through our expression of it in fellowship, in worship, and in service with other people of the faith.

We pray for peace on earth and for love among all people, but before we can ever have a world family, we have home families, and out of that home family comes love for other people.

A home that considers itself to be Christian will not only unite with other Christians in worship in the church, but will find ways of acknowledging God in the home. Family worship can never be overemphasized in importance, and as the Christian family becomes a worshiping family, it grows into a serving family in the community. The Christian home expresses itself in worship and service and becomes the most persuasive evangelizing agency in all the world. More converts are won to Christ in Christian homes than are won in all the churches put together.

> *The mutual assimilation and adjustment of the in-laws is not always easy. Anything that can serve to further the process is worth trying. What hinders process is worth avoiding.*

> HENRY A. BOWMAN
> Marriage for Moderns

> *Most parents at some time or other experience a sense of wonder, a glow of satisfaction, as they contemplate the idea of their own continuing life through the sons and daughters whom they have brought into the world.*

> DAVID R. MACE
> Whom God Hath Joined

> *The family thus becomes the true theater of goodness, because nowhere else can the identification of my interest with the interest of others be either so complete or so natural.*

> W. F. LOFTHOUSE
> Ethics and the Family

A married couple who love their home, their family, and their friends, create a charmed circle and make a warmth which radiates all it touches.

MARY MACAULEY

The sacred fire of domestic love, kindled from the altar of divine love, shall be carried far and wide into the world of human life.

HENSLEY   HENSON
Christian Marriage

6 Steps to Happiness in Marriage

Heaven is not reached at a single bound;
But we build the ladder by which we rise
From the lowly earth to the vaulted skies,
And we mount to its summit round by round.

JOSIAH GILBERT HOLLAND
From *"Gradatim"*

A marriage may be a masterpiece, a mixture or a muddle. Most marriages are mixtures, too many are muddles and some tragedies. A marriage rests on the love of a man and woman, and the kind of people they are.

The things that make marriage a muddle are the things that make life itself a muddle. Only in marriage they are more acutely felt, because marriage is the most consecrated form of human fellowship. It is a school of character, a test of living, and only adults should undertake it.

JOSEPH FORT NEWTON

Attaining a meaningful marriage relationship, for most people, is the most important thing in all life. Success in marriage is more important than success in business or society or any other relationships. Of course we know that the "ideal marriage" is not one without problems. The problem may be small; the prob-

37

lem may be big. We know better than to ask to have no problems—instead we ask for strength and wisdom and love to handle the problems as they come.

Marriages take place for many reasons: to get away from home, to assert the fact that one is an adult, to give a legitimate name to a baby, to gain social advantage, to gain material advantage, or because it is something one is expected to do. We cannot call these valid reasons for marriage. Sometimes marriage for "the wrong reasons" can be rescued and made into marriage for the "right reason." However the ideal marriage creates a union—spiritual, emotional, physical—in which two people become welded together as husband and wife. "... A man leaves his father and his mother and cleaves to his wife, and they become one flesh" (Genesis 2:24 RSV). "... The two shall become one.... So they are no longer two but one flesh" (Matthew 19:5, 6 RSV). At the very outset it is extremely important to believe—really believe—that real marriage is possible.

Realizing that "heaven is not reached at a single bound" and that marriage is really not accomplished in just the few moments of a ceremony, as beautiful and exciting as that ceremony may be, then perhaps we had better set ourselves to the task of climbing.

Turn Monologue Into Dialogue
Useless Words
So long as we speak the same language and never understand each other,
So long as the spirals of our words snarl and interlock
And clutch each other with the irreckonable gutterals,
Well ...

CARL SANDBURG

If the nations of the earth could and would communicate freely and openly and honestly, that would truly be the first step, and maybe the only step needed, to have peace on earth. The same thing is true in nearly every human relationship—certainly it is true in marriage. Real dialogue is hard for many people. Some are introverts by nature, particularly when they are at home. Sometimes people talk to themselves and forget there is anybody else around. Sometimes people think, but the words never come out, and like good intentions, thoughts just are not good enough.

Television may be the major block to communication in the home today. Many years ago couples and families sat by the fireside and talked or read. Today the television set shouts forth five, six, or even seven hours a day in most homes. Frequently, as one arrives home in the evening the television immediately must be turned on so the news can be heard. Husband and wife have favorite programs during the week; often she has her programs, and he has his, so she sits in the bedroom, and he sits in the den. Sunday afternoons, once a time for rides in the country and visiting friends, have become devoted to the ball game, and nothing is permitted to interfere.

Many couples only communicate unhappy, confused, or negative feelings. When they think in terms of "talking it over," they are thinking of some problem that needs to be solved; thus they become constantly on the defensive, each seeking to make his or her point. In that condition, the idea is to see which one can win out.

When a couple finds they are doing this, they need to engage, not in an argument, but in a discussion about something they both like. What a supporting experience for each! But tragically, many couples have so little in common to talk about. They follow the observation that "Love and nothing else soon becomes—nothing else."

For good communication to exist, there must be dialogue, not monologue. What is the difference? Take the example of the very sad little boy who said one day, "Mama won't ever let me say anything." Like many others in our society—preachers and teachers, doctors and judges, even husbands and wives—this boy's mother was probably ready to give the answer without even hearing the question. Such an attitude follows the rule "Don't confuse me with questions or facts; my mind is already made up." In monologue one person talks—and often no one listens; in dialogue two people both talk and listen. But real listening requires more than one's physical presence. While there in body, the "listener" may easily wander mentally. He may daydream, glance at a book or magazine or newspaper. That can hardly help communication.

But paying close attention to what your spouse says may bring unexpected benefits. Often just knowing that one has been heard brings satisfaction. The other may not really require a solution, just a simple, "I do hear you. I understand."

There are various other elements involved in communication. The real communicator has the ability to express feeling and to "hear" hidden meanings behind words. Inflections of the voice, implications, and emotions may change the meaning of words. Posture, voice inflection, facial expressions, what is not said, things like a wink or a tear—all may add meaning to otherwise confusing (or confuse otherwise clear) conversation. In describing influences on communication, Douglas Steere said, in *On Listening to Another*, "In conversation between two people there are at least six people present: what each person says are two; what each person meant to say are two more; what each person understood the other to say are two more."

How can we achieve good communication? Here let us consider some "helpful hints":

1. Ask the right questions. The husband who says, "Did you have a good day?" may get a "no" from his wife, and that may be the end of the conversation. Learn to ask I-want-to-listen questions. "Tell me about your day" may not sound like a question, but it can lead to more conversation.

2. Bring up the right questions at the right time. There are such things as being too tired, having headaches, and being absorbed in a book or television program. Communication will be easier if you choose the proper time.

3. Drop the preface. Comments such as "I am going to say...," or, "Let's talk seriously...," or, "I want you to listen to something..." may lose the thought. Just say it!

4. Talk one at a time, letting the other person get in his or her comments.

5. Don't talk too much. An insecure person may seek to overcome insecurities by talking and talking and talking, saying far more than needs to be said. Another tactic may be *intensifying*; that is, exaggerating one's feelings to get more attention.

Communication is the life-blood of all personal existence. It is essential to one's whole being as breathing is to his body. Awareness of this basic human situation has prompted penal officers and outlaws alike to devise solitary confinement as the most rigorous kind of punishment. All evidence points to the truth that the functional unit of a healthy humanity is not the lone individual but the community of two or more persons engaged in a variety of expressions of personal communications with each other. By the same token, the "iron curtain" is a symptom of a most deadly disease. It threatens the very existence of mankind in every generation. To be someone is to be in communication with someone else. To be alone, completely alone, is hell. The problem is fundamentally spiritual, and roots in the failure of communication between our spirits.

ALLEN O. MILLER
Theology and Life

Until Debt Us Do Part

We know that in the ceremony the word is *death*, but the truth of the matter is *debt* parts people a lot more quickly than death. Right off the bat, young couples want to begin living on the scale to which they have been accustomed. Their fathers and mothers worked long years to obtain the standard of living that they know and enjoy, but young people forget that. They are used to wearing certain kinds of clothes and driving a certain car and living in a certain type of house. It can be easily observed that when couples have made a living on their own for a period of time before marriage, they find themselves adjusting much more easily to the financial demand in marriage.

They are planning to get married,
I am rather glad they are.
Although the road ahead seems difficult and far.
They've very little money, and I am rather pleased at that;
They will know the joy of starving in an inexpensive flat.

Launching out together with high hopes and courage great.
They dream of just their salaries every week,
And they'll have to save and struggle now for every joy they seek.

Their bills will give them trouble, and they'll sigh for things in vain
She's going to do the cooking, and I fancy 'twill be plain.
He'll help her in the kitchen, and he'll dry the dishes too,
And learn a lot of duties which he never thought he'd do.

But every chair they purchase will be laden with delight;
Every trinket toiled and saved for will with joy be doubly bright.
So I'm not the least bit sorry, but am positively glad
For they'll know the fun of striving which their dad and mother had.

THEODORE F. ADAMS
Making Your Marriage Succeed

It will always remain true that "the best things in life are free." However these so-called "best things" do not pay the rent and the utilities and the grocery bill, buy clothes and furniture and all the other things that only money can pay for.

At this point, young married couples really do not get the sympathetic understanding from their parents that they deserve. Parents have a tendency to remember when they started, and they often equate the situation today as it was back then. Someone has figured out that forty to fifty years ago, when a couple started out to build a home together, they had about 119 wants, and of those, 17 were absolute necessities. Today there are 973 wants, and 117 necessities. Glass shower doors, electric washers and driers, TV sets, tape recorders, club memberships, and so forth, are relatively new upon the scene. A generation ago, there was more cooking done in the kitchen. Today expensive "quick" meals that take very little time cooking can be bought at the store. In this world of fast pace and fast food, a microwave oven seems an absolute necessity. Habits and attitudes we have grown up with are hard to change.

To begin with, a couple needs to realize that there are many different ways to handle their money, and any of those ways are good, just as long as the couple agrees on them. Today many couples both work. They may keep separate bank accounts, divide their expenses, with each one assuming certain responsibilities. Or they may put their money together and share their expenditures as they go. Or one or the other might be the "financial manager" of the family. The important thing is that they decide how they want to manage and learn to live with that decision.

Let me give you a personal illustration. When I married, I had an old car which had about run its course. Soon afterward, my wife and I decided that we had to have a new car, so we bought one on the installment plan. Paying for that car is where we got our idea of eternity. Month by month, the bill would come for that car payment, and we would bravely struggle to make it. Finally came one of the greatest days either of us had ever known. We sent in the last payment for that car. It really was a day of great joy and relief. After we had mailed that payment, we sat down together and made a rule that we kept from then on. We decided that we would never buy anything else on credit. We never violated that principle. If we could not pay for it, we did without. It is absolutely amazing how much we can do without.

Of course, when we were talking about "credit," we were not talking about investments. If you buy a home that you can afford, that really is not a debt, but an investment. You have an asset to equal your debt, and as long as you can reasonably make the payments, you are in good shape. We thought more of debt in reference to things you can eat up and wear out. It makes a tremendous difference when one takes the cash out of his or her pocket and pays for goods. Something about handing over cash is very sobering. We find it easier to write checks than to pay cash. And easier still is it to use those devilish credit cards. My wife and I never had a gasoline credit card. When we bought gas, we paid cash. We never held up a line in the grocery store by writing a check. We had the money to pay for our groceries. Credit cards can be very misleading and damaging. What difference does it make if a couple pays fifty dollars or sixty dollars for some item, if it is going to be charged on a credit card? But if you are going to lay out the cash, that extra ten dollars makes a difference.

Here is a good poem to memorize:

> *When maw gets out the monthly bills*
> *And sets them all in front of dad,*
> *She makes us children run and play*
> *Because she knows he might get mad.*

Spending can be a lot of fun, but paying bills can be calamity.

We read all kinds of books about making and keeping budgets and other records, but budgets can be a terrible burden. The easiest way to make the most of your money is to live by the principle "If we cannot pay for it, we can do without it."

There are some real good marriage money rules, such as:

> Work on paying the bills together—then each one knows where the money is going.
>
> Keep the checkbook balanced.
>
> Decide together how much you need to keep in your "emergency fund." When you use some for an emergency, be certain you replace it.
>
> Have a regular program of savings, and each month be fair to your savings account.
>
> Decide together on your major purchases, even on as many of minor purchases as possible.
>
> If you do not have the money, you cannot afford it. Then forget it.

Recognize the difference between "necessities" and "luxuries." Under luxuries many things can be listed, such as: eating out, vacation trips, entertainment, extra clothes, pets, another chair, and hobbies. Necessities are those things we have to have. It is amazing how small that list can be made. A couple can be happy together on very little. No couple can be happy with debt, debt, debt hanging over their heads. If one or both have parents or grandparents who want to share the financial needs of a couple, accept the gift with joy and be sure, very sure, that you express your genuine and heartfelt thanks. Usually one should express thanks verbally and then, soon after, with a written note. Don't take the silly attitude, "We make our way, and we do not want any help." That is selfish because it might be denying the joy of giving to someone who loves deeply. It takes grace to give and grace to receive.

At the other end of the spectrum, some couples seek to make their marriage COD—and *c*all *o*n *d*ad! But dad and mom usually know how to take care of themselves.

Now that we've spoken of the grace of giving, this is a good place to think about your own giving. The young couple who learns to give early in their marriage opens the door to blessings. We need to learn to give to each other in the very beginning, and truly we need to learn to give to God. Marriage is really a spiritual experience, and the couple that leaves the church and the Bible and God out of their life cheats themselves. Even though you have very little, you need early in your marriage to develop the habit of giving together. Give to your church. Give to certain charities in your community. Giving expands and enlarges and tones up a person's life. Be careful that your possessions do not possess you—that what you own does not eventually own you.

Ask yourself these two questions, and as you give the answers you are well on the road to fiscal responsibility:

1. What is your most expensive luxury?
2. What percentage of your income do you give?

The dollar bill has sometimes been called "homemaker or breaker" number one. It is true that arguments arise quickly between husband and wife if there is misunderstanding about money. A court judge has reported: "Quarrelling about money is a major reason for America's unprecedented divorce rate. It is difficult to over-estimate the vicious part financial trouble is playing in the American home." In one study it was discovered that young husbands attributed 48% of their most serious marital problems to financial difficulty.

JOHN CHARLES WYNN
How Christian Parents
Face Family Problems

Marry Your Spouse's Family, Too

Every so often, a young married person will say, "I married him [or I married her], but I did not marry his [or her] family." Those are stupid and silly words. Your spouse's family is an inseparable part of him or her. You should neither expect nor desire the one you marry to immediately forget mother and father, sisters and brothers, aunts and uncles, and all the rest. When you marry a person, you marry the entire person, and family is a part of every normal and happy person. If couples expect to get along with each other, they must learn to get along with each other's family.

Of course, when two people marry, the families, especially the parents, have a very important obligation. In a very real sense, when the parents consent to the marriage, they also consent to the son or daughter having the freedom to build his or her own home. It is not easy for parents to "let go," and in a sense, parents never let go. They continue to love their son or daughter. Marriage means separation in many ways, but certainly parents continue to love their children. However, their love is not a controlling love. They want their children to take their own places in society as responsible men and women and to build their own homes. There should never be any conflict between the homes of the parents and the homes of their children.

However, in every marriage there must be some "laws for in-laws." To begin with, the first priority of the husband and the wife is to each other and no in-law—mother, father, brother, sister—ever takes priority. Read again these words of Jesus:

> *Have ye not read, that he which made them at the beginning made them male and female, and said, For this cause shall a man leave father and mother, and shall cleave to his wife: and they twain shall be one flesh? Wherefore, they are no more twain, but one flesh. . . . What therefore God hath joined together, let no man put asunder.*

> *Matthew 19:4–6*

To leave "father and mother" does not mean to quit appreciating, loving, visiting, having fellowship; what it means is our first loyalty and our first love belong to the one we marry. Both children and parents must—*must*—recognize this.

Really, this should never be a problem. We love our parents; then we come to love another person, and we marry that person; later a baby is born into our home, and we love that baby. There are three loves; none diminishing the others, and none in conflict with the others.

One of the first things a couple needs to do is to give their parents and parents in-law a title. Decide what you are going to call them. One of the couple should not refer to the parents of the other as "your dad" or "your mother." Get a name that you are comfortable with, be it *father, papa, dad, mother, mama,* or whatever. Oftentimes, the parents can be very helpful at this point and can suggest to the in-law what they would like to be called. However, generally, it is better to call your parents in-law the same thing your spouse calls them.

Remember that as you marry, you should "put away childish things," and you should take responsibility for your action. Do not blame your failures and your faults on your parents, and do not blame the failures or the faults of your spouse on his or her parents. Stand on your own two feet.

One of the Ten Commandments states, "Honor thy father and thy mother." One way to do this is to draw upon their wisdom and experience. Our parents have lived longer than we have; they have had experience we have not had. In these areas their knowledge is greater. We cheat ourselves when we do not draw upon the wisdom and advice of our parents. We are not controlled by their thoughts, because we remain free to make our own decisions. Recognizing our own freedom, we need not feel threatened by the attitudes of our parents and parents in-law.

Couples should never forget that parents have worries and fears. They see one whom they have known and loved from birth going out of their lives and their homes, and sometimes they feel real fear.

With their nest empty, many parents face older years, retirement, fear of living alone, and the thought of death. They need the support that their children can give. We think about what parents can do for their children. However, sometimes a mother likes to be taken out to lunch or have a birthday remembrance or receive letters and pictures and occasionally to sit with her child at church.

Brothers and sisters, as they build their own homes, should become more than brothers and sisters—they should become good friends and should share fun times together.

Marriage enlarges a person and gives him or her more grandparents, aunts, uncles, cousins, and a greater stake in life. Relatives should be a real benefit.

A wonderful and physical tie binds the parents to the children; and—by sad, strange irony—it does not bind us children to our parents. For if it did, if we could have their love not with gratitude, but with equal love, life would lose much of its pathos, much of its squalor, and we might be wonderfully happy.

E. M. FORSTER
Where Angels Fear to Tread

Too much privacy and we won't have anyone with whom to remember, let alone with whom to make plans. Too much individualism and we forget not only our ancestors and our possible descendants, but even each other.

JANE HOWARD
Families

Five More Ingredients for a Happy Marriage

These little steps can be very important in making a marriage happy.

1. Keep the romance going. In many couples, one or both partners see marriage as the end of romance, rather than the beginning.

It is so easy to get busy, to get up in the morning and rush through breakfast and hurry to work, to come home in the afternoon, do the chores. We have to live with the telephones, radios, doorbells, the daily mail, the newspapers, television. Then as time goes on there are children. We remember the old saying, "Man works from sun to sun, but a woman's work is never done."

Every couple must spend some time in a quiet, romantic, nondefensive setting. We need to be able to talk and hold each other's hands, express our joys and our hurts, to tune in with each other's spirits. We begin marriage as two personalities, and we are very different people. To begin with, we are male and female, and because of this, we think and feel and react differently. We do not regret that we are different. But as we live together we learn to adjust to each other and with each other, to give and take, and gradually to move toward each other.

Misunderstandings, quarrels, even hard feelings will occur in a marriage. But just as broken bones can be healed, so can broken feelings. However, the battle between *me* and *thee* can become destructive. It was Martin Luther who once said, "Between husband and wife there should be no question between *me-um* and *te-um* [mine and thine]."

2. *Remember thankfulness and thoughtfulness.* Relationships begin to slide downhill when we begin to take each other for granted. If one has done something nice for the other, be sure not only to notice it, but to express appreciation and thankfulness. One of the sweetest expressions in human relations is "thank you."

3. *We must mind our manners.* When we are with other people, we give more attention to politeness, but when we go in the house and close the door, we may feel inclined to leave our manners outside. When we think of it, we know and no one needs to tell us that it is not good to be more polite with every one else than with the one whom we marry and whom we love the most. Manners mean courtesy, consideration, helpfulness, and a lot of little things that make one appreciated.

4. *Make mutual friends.* During courtship and after the wedding, couples remain very much preoccupied with each other. Their supreme desire is to be left alone, and they are only vaguely aware of people around them. The honeymoon is the most private of all occasions. Throughout the early period of married life, couples desire seclusion. But as they settle down together, they realize that isolation cannot fulfill their marriage. In their new home they realize the importance of both social obligations and social opportunities. Families cannot be complete within themselves. They need fellowship with other families; they need to know the meaning of being good neighbors, and

at times the door of each home must open toward people in the community.

The very best time to make friends is as couples are just starting out. If you wait too long, you will find that couples your age have already made friends of long standing, and it is difficult for newcomers to be included. In the church, the office, the neighborhood—wherever people meet—get to know others. Howard and Charlotte Clinebell, in *The Intimate Marriage*, said "Over-investment in a marriage increases the mutual demand load and puts a dangerous emotional blight on both husband and wife."

The husband will have his friends, and the wife will have hers; however it is very important that they share some mutual friends.

Duel or Duet

One husband said, "My wife and I have lived together forty-five years and never had a cross word." In reply, someone said, "He has either lived a dull life or has a poor memory." The truth is, two real people, no matter how much they love each other, will have some "duels."

Some areas of conflict may include:

Money
Not being able to really talk to each other
Attitudes toward members of each other's family
Likes and dislikes—choosing clothes, furniture, a car, a house—wherever there are choices, conflicts may occur
Division of work around the house
Choices of entertainment

Time and again married couples need to remember that, "the path of true love never runs smoothly."

Some feel that conflicts in marriage are primarily due to the fact that one is male and the other is female. Certainly very basic differences exist between male and female. But more often those differences support and supplement each other, rather than create conflict. Two women living together or two men living together could have differences that could lead to dissension and unhappiness. Couples should realize they must understand and adjust to each other. Use of expressions such as "that is just like a woman" or "that is just like a man" is really not valid. There are differences in men and women, but there are also differences between any two women and between two men. Each person is a separate personality; differences should be expected, and, in fact, at times they are good, because through differences we often experience deep and real communication.

Since there are bound to be some real duels along with our duets, let us here list some of the basic rules to go by:

1. Decide the basic issue. This is the most important step in any difference between husband and wife. In fact, when both agree on the real issue, many times the fight is over. Often we really do not know what we are fighting about. So very soon after the couple gets into the "boxing ring," let one or the other ask the question, "What are we really fighting about?" Most of the time, that question goes a long way toward settling the problem. Define the issue first.

2. Consider the circumstances at the moment. Does one or the other feel tired or sick, or is one depressed because of something that happened on the job today, or does one feel worried about a family member, and so on. Sometimes one or the other is emotionally drained or physically tired. That is not the time to have a good fight. Timing is important, and it is better to wait than to make the problem worse.

3. Deal with the issue before you now. One of the dangers in married fights is to become "historical." That is, to go back and bring up everything that has ever happened in the past. We gain nothing by constantly fighting over yesterday. The problems of today are sufficient, and we need to deal with them. In our duels from time to time we need to raise the question "Are we dealing with the issue today or are we rehashing something of yesterday?"

4. We have already decided what the issue is and that this is the right time to discuss it; let us stick to the issue. That in itself requires real discipline, but it helps us come to understanding conclusions.

5. Keep it under control. Arguments overshadowed by anger never really accomplish anything and most of the time make things worse. Shouting, crying, sulking, throwing things, cursing, refusing to talk— these and similar actions do not accomplish what we desire, and they cause things to happen that we do not want to occur. Lack of self-control

often leads to more problems than the original issues. We always need to remember that temper does not improve with use.

6. Keep it private. Some things between husband and wife should not be shared with parents, friends, children, or anybody else. There are some things, both happy and unhappy, that should be kept strictly between the two. Most of the time telling somebody else does harm. The old saying "Do not wash your dirty laundry in public" certainly applies to marriage. Embarrassing each other is very unthoughtful and unloving.

7. Keep your discussion completely within the realm of truth. Be honest in whatever you say. Untruths eventually entrap one and make the situation worse. It may be that some things do not need to be said. But let us be sure that whatever is said is the truth. There is an ancient prayer:

> From the cowardice that shrinks from new truth,
> From the laziness that is content with half truths,
> From the arrogance that thinks it knows all truth,
> O God of *truth*, deliver us.

8. Fights between couples are very serious and should be considered so. Still it does not hurt to smile occasionally, and it does not hurt to use an occasional bit of humor. Each of us wishes to be taken seriously, and for one or the other to sit there with a silly grin on his or her face is not good, but real humor can sometimes lessen the tension and increase the communication.

Charles Dickens once said, "While there is infection in disease and sorrow, there is nothing in the world quite so irresistibly contagious as laughter and good humor." Seriousness and humor are not contradictions—they supplement and support each other.

9. Let us ask ourselves, "What is the purpose of this fight?" There really can be only one legitimate purpose, and that is to settle something. If we fight just to hurt each other or to embarrass each other, to inflate our own egos or to give vent to our own frustrations, then we make a very serious and sad mistake. If the thing we are concerned about cannot be brought to some reasonable resolution, then we are far more than wasting our time, we are hurting each other and accomplishing no good.

Real advantages exist in a good fight; we bring problems out into the open, deal with them, and settle them. In your fights do not go too far. Never get physical. There is absolutely no excuse for a husband or a wife to physically attack the other one. That action lies beneath human dignity and should never happen. Neither should one try to belittle another's emotions or show a lack of respect. In spite of the problem, let us continue to hold each other in a sense of appreciation and respect. Let us avoid accusation. Never rush out of the house or "go home to mama." Stay together, and when the problem is too big, remember there is always professional help available. Stop before you leave scars and remember that hard things spoken can live in the mind and heart of the other one forever. If you do not mean it, do not say it.

Settle it. This is really the main reason for the argument in the first place. Remember the important thing is not for one to win and for one to lose. The benefits come from issues defined, discussed, understood, and settled. Self-confidence must never be destroyed. Self-image must be maintained. Never use bluffs. Going in a room and closing the door solves nothing. I grew up in a home with seven children and a very wise and loving mother and father. My father had a very basic rule that I never knew him to break. That rule was that, if anything happened between parents and one of the children or between two of the children, we would not go to bed that night until we settled it. I can remember we sometimes sat up rather late at night, but we stayed with it until my father decided it was settled.

The other part of that rule was that after it was settled it would never be mentioned again. I never knew my father or mother to violate that. They never would say, "You remember when you . . ." and bring up something unhappy or bitter. When it was settled, it was settled.

Saint Paul said, ". . . Let not the sun go down upon your wrath" (Ephesians 4:26). That statement may have more meaning for us than we first realize. Many times our fights take place at night, and as we go further into the night we get wearier and wearier and our spirits become worse and worse. It might be a good idea to settle our differences before sundown, then eat dinner and go to bed together happily. Anyway, the issue needs to be settled, and when it is settled, left alone.

I bind myself for life! I have chosen: From now on my aim
will be, not to search for someone who may please me, to please

the one I have chosen. This decision can alone produce a successful marriage, and if the vow is not sincere, the couple's chances for happiness are very slim, for it will run the risk of disruption when the first obstacles and the inevitable difficulties of life in common are encountered.

ANDRE MAUROIS
The Art of Living

The kindest and the happiest pair
Will find occasion to forebear,
And something, every day they live,
To pity, and, perhaps, forgive.

WILLIAM COWPER

If you forgive people enough, you belong to them, and they to you, whether either person likes it or not—squatters rights of the hearts.

JAMES HILTON

I have made a ceaseless effort not to ridicule, not to bewail, not to scorn human actions, but to understand them.

BARUCH SPINOZA

Consider the hammer—it keeps its head.
It doesn't fly off the handle.
It keeps pounding away.
It finds the point and then drives it home.
It looks at the other side, too,
And thus often clinches the matter.
It makes mistakes, but when it does it starts all over.
It is the only knocker in the world
That does any good.

ANONYMOUS

We who have been taught to "forgive our enemies" surely should have learned to forgive our dearest loved ones.

7 The Home in the House

When couples marry, one of the exciting experiences is having a place of their own. It may be an apartment or a house. Often, to start with, they do not have the money to buy all the furniture they want, or maybe they can't even have the type of furniture they desire. However, fixing up that first place becomes an exciting and wonderful experience. As time goes by they think in terms of upgrading their house. It is said that the average couple moves two or three times before they reach the "house level" they really want. Don't make some couples' great mistake of buying a house that costs more than you can afford. That can be a heavy burden.

Once a couple whose marriage ceremony I had performed invited me to have dinner at their house. As I stopped on the street in front of their house, I was greatly impressed with it. It stood in a nice neighborhood and seemed such an attractive building. The couple met me at the door and as we went in one of them said, "You will notice we do not have any furniture in the dining room or the living room." We went on into the den, and they had some chairs, but they were not elegant. In the bedroom they showed me a big, foam-rubber mattress on the floor, but very little bedroom furniture. In explanation they told me how they had heard me say that debt could be a heavy burden. They carefully figured how much they could afford to pay in house payments, and they bought a house on that level, but they said that they would wait until they could afford furniture, and they would buy it as they went along. That made good sense to me.

Likewise, you start off together building a home. But the home is not visible when the marriage is over. Whatever the house is, the home can be built inside, and we need to keep in mind that more important than the house, is the home.

Often, we see signs HOME FOR SALE. You cannot buy a home. You can buy a house that is already built; you can buy materials and build a house; but you *must* build your home, and no one else can do it for you.

To begin with, the home represents the closest relationship two people can have. Probably the fear of being alone is the deepest fear that any person has. Loneliness becomes a great burden.

The home is built on the loving fellowship of the husband and the wife. Later, children come, and their presence creates a family. Parents and children share a wonderful relationship. But the day comes when the children are gone and the parents remain. When the children leave, they do not take their home with them; their home stays with the parents, and the children go out and start the process of building a new home.

Really and truly, that relationship between husband and wife is really the home, which should begin at marriage and should continue to grow as long as they live.

An old story tells of a couple who had lived together many, many years. Now in their old age both were nearly deaf and could only hear each other with difficulty. One night they sat before the fireside together. He kept looking across the table at her, thinking about all the things she had done for him through the years. But he had never been one to express his love, and he had taken all her goodness and favors rather for granted. That night he felt a sudden inspiration, and he said to her, "I am proud of you." And she looked across at him and replied, "I am tired of you, too." Happily, in most marriages, couples do not get "tired" of each other. Instead they become more and more a part of each other. Many couples who have lived together harmoniously through many years not only tend to think alike, they actually come to look alike physically.

Couples need to enjoy sharing all their experiences together—both their joys and their sorrows. At a lovely banquet where a very distinguished man had received high honor, he responded, "I appreciate this honor, but really it does not mean very much to me now. You see, my wife died last year, and now I have nobody to tell it to." The greatest dread we have about death is not so much leaving this life, not so much the fear of the next life, but the fact that we must take this one journey alone. Death would not be nearly such a dreaded experience if it could be taken with human companionship. Joys are much greater and sorrows are much less when they are shared. Talk to persons whose loved one has died, and you will hear them saying that during their moments of deepest sorrow they yearn for the fellowship and companionship of the one with whom they have walked through the years.

One of the first things married couples must learn is that marriage is not the same as courtship. When a couple had a "date," each one was dressed for the occasion, and each was prepared to give full and complete attention to the other. On a date couples are much more likely to be concerned about the feelings and desires and joys of the other one. They want to make it a very happy and wonderful occasion.

Marriage can be and should be a lifelong love affair. We realize that every marriage includes the routines of living: hurrying to get ready for work, housework, going to the grocery store, taking care of the yard, washing clothes and the dishes, and all the necessary common tasks. However the sharing in marriage can be—and for many, many couples is—the source of the greatest joys in life.

A saying tells us, "We do not marry the one we love, we learn to love the one we marry." Most people today do marry the one they love and happily they realize as they go along that it is necessary to keep on learning to love the one they marry. The idea that marriages are "made in heaven" is beautiful but unreal. A person could marry any one of many and be happy because, really and truly, the couple builds the deeper foundations of marriage after the ceremony. There will be adjustments to make and difficulties to overcome. The joy of fellowship must be cultivated, and couples must learn to accept and respect each other as individuals and treat each other as equals. In marriage, couples must remain constantly aware of the danger of one or the other dominating or exploiting the other. Before one makes a decision, opinions and feelings of the other must be considered. Marriage involves both a partnership and a love relationship. As partners, couples learn to share the responsibility and the duties as well as the privileges. And in the love relationship they find stimulating and satisfying unity. A couple realizes that masculine and feminine differences exist, and these very differences attract each other and fill their hearts with loving gratitude. Marriage is both utilitarian and romantic. Each partner brings to the marriage relationship an accumulation of experiences, attitudes, habits, opinions, goals, and ideals. Couples do not naturally want to be exactly alike in every area of life. But as they constantly make adjustments they develop their own strengths and characters.

In marriage there are moments when anger will become very evident, and when bitter words will be spoken, and when deceit will be used. Happily, we learn that loving understanding and forgiveness can be very real.

If we remember the saying, "Love and nothing else soon becomes—nothing else," we will have better marriages. The strongest marriages include "a third loyalty." When I was a very young minister in a rural church, I once had a "testimony meeting"—a time when people would stand and tell their experiences. In one of these meetings a very simple rural farmer stood up and said, "When I was a little boy, I loved my mother, and I felt that I would never love anybody else but my mother. Years went by, and I met this lovely girl, and I fell in love with her. Then I felt I would never love anyone else but my mother and the girl I married. Later, a little baby girl was born into our home, and I loved her. And now I loved my mother and my wife and my daughter. Then one day, I met Jesus Christ, made a commitment of my life, and I found that after I came to love Jesus, I not only loved my mother and my wife and daughter, but then, I realized I loved everybody else."

> *A house is built of logs and stones,*
> *Of tiles and posts and piers;*
> *A home is built of loving deeds*
> *That stand a thousand years.*

>   *VICTOR HUGO*

> *Our fathers had a saying about marriage, that if two people ride on a horse, one of the two must ride behind. Today marriage is more like two people riding abreast on the same horse, doing a rather difficult balancing feat and each holding one*

rein. It's more companionable than the old way, but it's more complicated, and must at times be rather confusing to the horse.

LORD BEVERIDGE

The man is restless while he misses his rib that was taken out of his side; and the woman is restless till she gets under the man's arm, from whence she was taken.

RABBINIC SAYING

Unless religion be at home in the house, no amount of religion in the temple *can save us.*

E. STANLEY JONES

A dramatist named Alfred Sutrau once wrote a fine, if forgotten, play called A Maker of Men, *in which a bank clerk returns home, after missing a promotion and says, "I see other men getting on; what have I done?"*
His wife answered; "You have made a woman love you. You have given me respect for you, and admiration, and loyalty, and devotion—everything a man could give his wife, except luxury, and that I don't need. Still you call yourself a failure, who within these four walls are the greatest success?"

CHANNING POLLOCK

"It takes a heap o' livin' in a house t' make it home."

EDGAR A. GUEST

'Mid pleasures and palaces though we may roam,
Be it ever so humble, there's no place like home;
A charm from the skies seems to hallow us there,
Which, sought through the world is ne'er met with elsewhere.

Home, home, sweet, sweet home,
Be it ever so humble there's no place like home.

JOHN HOWARD PAYNE

8 Wisdom From the Wisest Book

And Adam said, This is now bone of my bones, and flesh of my flesh: she shall be called Woman, because she was taken out of Man. Therefore shall a man leave his father and his mother, and shall cleave unto his wife: and they shall be one flesh. And they were both naked, the man and his wife, and were not ashamed.

Genesis 2:23–25

And Jesus answered and said unto them, For the hardness of your heart he wrote you this precept. But from the beginning of the creation God made them male and female. For this cause shall a man leave his father and mother, and cleave to his wife; And they twain shall be one flesh: so then they are no more twain, but one flesh. What therefore God hath joined together, let not man put asunder.

Mark 10:5–9

Whoso findeth a wife findeth a good thing, and obtaineth favour of the Lord.

Proverbs 18:22

Love suffereth long, and is kind; love envieth not; love vaunteth not itself, is not puffed up, Doth not behave itself unseemly, seeketh not her own, is not easily provoked, thinketh no evil; Rejoiceth not in iniquity, but rejoiceth in the truth; Beareth all things, believeth all things, hopeth all things, endureth all things.

See *1 Corinthians 13:4–7*

To every thing there is a season, and a time to every purpose under the heaven: A time to be born, and a time to die; a time to plant, and a time to pluck up that which is planted; A time to kill, and a time to heal; a time to break down, and a time to build up; A time to weep, and a time to laugh; a time to mourn, and a time to dance; A time to cast away stones, and a time to gather stones together; a time to embrace, and a time to refrain from embracing; A time to get, and a time to lose; a time to keep, and a time to cast away; A time to rend, and a time to sew; a time to keep silence, and a time to speak; A time to love, and a time to hate; a time of war, and a time of peace.

Ecclesiastes 3:1–8